AMERICA'S BEST WINGZ!!

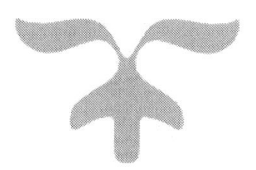

WRITTEN BY SHAWN YURINA RICHARDSON

FORWARD

Like a gift that keeps on giving, this compilation of Poems and Love Letters is one I enjoyed to NO end.

Shawn Yurina Richardson's seemingly raunchy and suggestive titles would make you become deep in thought to anticipate the fantasies contained within. On cautiously diving in, you're left in awe in his "classy fashion of writing" combined with a level of eroticism that leaves you yearning for more in such poems in this book like "Love letter" that talks about the taste of you.

The book praises the lover in such a way that it seamlessly maintains a balance on adoration without breaching the borders of exaggeration.

It's a lovely compilation with a scintillating language, transporting you into the world of the writer; a world of a man who loves, favors and admires his woman, who may or may not exist as of yet, but he waits.

Shawn's creative vocabulary in this treasure is one of the wins of this book. The writing leaves you enamoured at the ease of every powerful second which he

shows off and describes the kind of woman who would be be suitable for him.

Mr. Richardson has done a fine job in transitioning various themes to produce a master piece of classy sexual poetry that would leave any woman weak at the knees but also fondling.

To the one who holds this book, if you intend to offer this book as a gift, it's definitely going to be a memorable one and it could also serve as your secret love tool on days you seek ideas and thoughts that would make your partner swoon.

America's Best Wings!!

Love letters, Poetry and Chicken Wing Recipes.

BOLD
Assertive
Gentle
KiNg
Romantic
Fun
Out G
SpO

Organized
Totally Committed
Honorable
High Standards
Impeccable
Fit for Conquest
Heroic
Glory Builder
Energetic
High Profile
Dominant
Top Quality
Buttoned up
Over Achiever
Competitive
Superior Value
Excellence

Author: Shawn Yurina Richardson

About the Author

Shawn Yurina Richardson is a Prophet, Father, Mentor, Author, Singer and Motivational Speaker. As a Role Model and an Educator, he communicates sexual education in an unparallel manner. He brings an intimate level of sexual education to the forefront, that we can observe or see in the light of what Jesus Christ gave us to experience, within the laws of what He created.

The bond between husband and wife can be as weak or as powerful as what is understood by the two. In other words, the husband-wife bond cannot be stronger than their understanding. The only limitation is the lack of obedience to the Word of God or the lack of Information. Information in this sense is focused on the Word of God. The Word is God. The Word is with God. The Word is from God. Information is God. When you receive information from God, God is giving you Himself and this is exactly what he is set to do in your life through the pages of this book.

I command light to shine in your life. I shine the Light of the Word of God into your relationship and your marriage. Be enlightened from this intimate masterpiece.

Copyright

Copyright @ 2020 Shawn Yurina Richardson

The right of the author has been asserted to him in accordance with the

copyright writing, designs and patent act of the United States of America.

All rights reserved. No part of this book may be reproduced, stored or transmitted by any means whether auditory, graphic, mechanical, or electronic without the written permission of the author. Unauthorized reproduction of any part of this work is illegal and is punishable by law.

Unless otherwise noted, the author and the publisher make no explicit guarantees as the accuracy of the information contained in this book may differ based on individual experiences and context.

For enquiries: contact us at PunchPoetry@gmail.com

Table Of Contents

FORWARD 2
About the Author 5
Copyright 7
Ranch Dressing-Poem 11
The Letter - 1 17
A different truth 21
Cruise Control 24
Anxious to taste you 29
Balls Deep 33
Don't Worry 39
Spice your lyfe 47
Brown Sugar 49
Thoughts in Action 54
Fantasy Island 57
The God System 62
Fight Night 66
Who am I? 69
Tired of Thinking 75
Late in the night can be Late in Life 79
Sending you Flowers 84

My Love has No Expiration	88
Appointed for Sweetness	93
My mind is soaked	98
Freak Fest	105
I Need You	108
Round 3	116
Prioritize	118
White lies & white lives	121
Three, Two, One	130
Sixty Six Angels	133
Now	135
Access	138
A King's Love	142
Easy for life	146
War in a Bottle	149

(Poem1)

Ranch Dressing-Poem

Being appreciated is not always easy to do

Expectations can be disappointed

But appreciation was my strategy to become closer to you

Your eyes; your smile and the way you think

Has placed you in my arms

As I entered your heart, I began to sink

Am I sinking or falling?

Falling in love with you is my calling

Many are called but few are chosen

I'm just praying that the light in me doesn't lead me into

a dark place with you

Where I am not respectful or don't recognize how beautiful

You really are...to me
I think about spending the rest of my life
With a woman who I can call my wife
I don't want to think twice
I don't want to think at all
All I want to do is hold both hands with you
Running as fast as we can
As we both leap, off of a cliff
that is millions of miles in the air
Safety is the last thing on our mind
We don't care
We jumped off the tallest mountain
We're in the air. I hold you above my head
As I drink from your fountain.
Tasting purer than the purest of waters;
Feeding my soul, quenching my thirst
You're Clenching my arms to cum in my lungs
. You're speaking in tongues

Calm down. You accidentally ripped off my shirt
I'm in the air with you. I'm putting in work
Dominating you. You almost slipped but I grabbed you
by the throat and pulled you to me
This is where we are
Enjoying the opportunity
The vultures of our past can't get on our level
We're up in the air
Way above the clouds
And I have no plans of landing
This is a sky diving experience
I'm sky diving into you
Sky diving into the eyes of a woman so beautiful
Diving deep into the blissful oceans of your paradise
Deep into a place where I may not belong
But I want to be
I want to be so close to you that my spirit will have to
leave my body to meet you

I want to be with you deep

So deep that we don't think the same

Deeper until neither one of us remembers our name

Deep...

So deep that we forget to eat breakfast, lunch, and dinner

We make each other winners. We're not adolescent

We're professionals. Not beginners

Deep...

I want to bypass your lowercase g spot

To land on the capital G of your galaxy

How did I arrive there?

Spiritually

I took a different avenue to be with you

I went around your womb

I didn't bruise or put a scratch on your Celibacy

Everything is intact and remained the same

No harm done

Living life without blame

God has established you and I make you prosper in Jesus name

I'm a man that challenges you;

Making you excel, countless miles per hour.

The Letter - 1

Baby, don't play with me. This is the first altercation that we've ever had and I never want it to happen again. From now on, no more arguing. No more fussing and fighting. No more being dramatic about our disagreements with each other. No more escalation of negative vibes. It's not cool and if it happens again, I'm out of here! I will make sure that it will be the last day you see me. You will never hear from me, ever again. I'll move to a different country and be with someone else who understands and loves effective communication. All the time I share with you will be given to someone else. I cannot and will not allow myself to be in a position where you speak to me as if I'm worthless. You got me fucked up! You gonna learn today!! Obviously, I'm nothing like the guys you've dated. They may represent your past but I am the future. If you are ready to grow from here and put this stuff behind us, start with confessions. Who doesn't have faults? But if we can't apologize and admit our wrongs, how then can we open ourselves up to better character and behavior. Confession should be a daily part of our life. It exposes toxic things that have ruined individuals, marriages, businesses as well as corrupted powerful potentials of becoming greater. There is so much force in confession unfortunately, too many people are trying to gain the force of momentum by trying to act like they are perfect. You are wrong and if you really want me like you say you do, show me by your confession. Expose all of that mess so that we can get it out of the way to ensure it doesn't destroy this relationship. Then, we can proceed with the lifestyle that compliments what a healthy relationship is all about. I am only going to give you one last chance and if you accept me, you gotta follow me - we have to come together and become one unit. Hormonally, we have to be on the same mind and language. I'm going to be the vehicle but you need to be the gas. I'm going to be the gun but you're going to be the ammunition. It's either we do this together and win or be failures and not do it at all. What's your decision my darling?

(Poem 2)

A different truth

Baby, I don't always think before I speak
I admit there have been times I've said some dumb things
My occupation is selling my published books and signing photographs
My advocates enjoy taking pictures with me and asking for autographs!
At my book signing, there were so many people there
A few were asking tricky questions
I don't want to say something that leads someone into depression
I expected this event to last 2 to 3 hours
So many haters are waiting for me to put my foot in the wrong place

It was stressful but I still had fun

When I got home

Dinner was already DONE

In fact, it was cold because I couldn't finish working until much later than expected

I showered and came into the room to find I was arrested

You handcuffed me to each side of the bed rails and read me my rights

You were feeling frisky at 10:38 that night

So, I gave you what you wanted. Kids on the other side of the house

That didn't stop you from moaning

I had to cover your freaking mouth

I gave you more than you could handle

It's not your birthday but I'm blowing fire out of your candles!

Every time I blew, I heard the sound of a splash

I call you Dr. King because you are free at last

You got on top

Looked in my eyes and asked

What's wrong with you?

I had a long day

No need to summarize

...saying I was sleepy shouldn't be a surprise

It was a big mistake

...but I apologize

Please forgive me for telling you the truth.

(Letter 2)

Cruise Control

Hey sweetheart. I hope that when you receive this letter, you are in good health, feeling good, encouraged, and motivated. I'm writing this letter because I was reading the Bible earlier - Deuteronomy 8:18 which says:

But thou shalt remember the Lord thy God: for it is He that giveth thee power to get wealth, that He May establish His covenant which He has sworn unto thy fathers, as it is this day.

Sweetheart, as I was looking into this verse, I saw something that I didn't see before. I use to just see the part where God gives us the power to get wealth. So, what I realized is that it's not just me that has this power. It's not just you. It's us! Both of us! We have the power. My problem may have been that I was trying to become wealthy on my own. I generated lots of money over a period of time but it is nothing like what we can do together. That was the second part that I realized. The other light I saw is that wealth doesn't just come simply because God gave us power. It means he has enabled us. Baby, he gave us this ability. The ability is a gift but the gift of the ability is not just an idea to make money. This gift is activated simply by remembering God. That's the first thing he said: FOR THOU SHALT REMEMBER THE LORD THY GOD. How do we remember Him? We remember Him by Speaking what he said from out of our mouth, recalling it and rehearsing it in our mind. Every time we worship God, we are remembering Him. The other factor of God's given power is when we give our tithes and offerings. When we give our tithes, He rebukes the devourer of the air. Do you remember what happened to Job? The devourer went through everything that was his and barely left him with anything. Baby, the devourer of the air is an angel. To devour means to eat quickly. We don't see that angel with our physical eyes but what we do know is that it will come in quickly and take everything we have worked hard for. The tithe is only ten percent of what we earn. If a person has a million dollars and doesn't give God tithe from it, that million dollars wouldn't last longer than someone who only has ten dollars. This is a very serious matter. When we tithe our money, it allows us to maintain our possessions and enjoy the things we have. When we tithe our time and money, we are remembering God and in return, we're enjoying it, receiving more and we're maintaining what he has already given us.

So sweetheart, even though you can't see me right now, while you're reading this letter, I Am on one knee, proposing to you, to ask if you will tithe with me?

Imagine

I imagine you on your front porch, enjoying dinner with Thunder, Rain, and your blanket.
These are the names of people who have specific functionalities.
The front porch represents clearer skies and investments.
It's a place of meditation for assessments.
Thunder stimulates the emotions within yourself that when you speak,
you sound like the thunder of what you hear.
The force of gravity
and nature in itself is too much for one person to bear.
So you sit in that element and absorb the beauty that nature gives.
You give rain to flowers that you come in contact with.
Flowers reveal that you are beautiful
But they don't show you your true value.
So you wrap yourself in a blanket to allow your mind to go where your body can't.
You close your eyes and feel the wind's voice, blowing through the blanket to get to your bones.
Bones represent your soul.
Your soul represents your life.
Life represents our will.
Our will represents our thoughts.
Our thoughts represent where we are and who we want to be.
I wanted to be under that blanket with you.
I want to feel your energy.
I'm closer to you than I think
But sometimes I don't think I cant ever be close enough unless I become you and you become me.
I keep seeing things.
I saw something today.
It's the same thing I saw about 6 years ago, and I've been praying the same thing, saying...God, please.

Anxious to taste you

You want some chicken? Here you Go!!! I'm giving you some of my favorite recipes. I'm giving you the right to eat all the freaking chicken wings you damn well, please!

It's no secret to making these wings that are marinated, crispy, and delicious. Let these babies bask in the juices of the flavors and seasonings for an hour and a half. Here are the ingredients below but first, let me ask, what kind of woman do you have? Is she quiet? Is she shy? Is she loud and bossy? I want you to have her come over when you have about 30 minutes left of these wings to finish cooking.

Read one the next poems, that comes after this recipe and make sure you set your timer because the conversation may get deep and I don't want you to burn the wings. Set your timer and enjoy this experience that you are about to have. Enjoy!

10 – 12 chicken wings, skinless or skin-on

For the marinade

1/4 teaspoon paprika

1/4 teaspoon salt

1/2 cup all-purpose flour

1/4 teaspoon cayenne pepper or chili powder

For the hot sauce

1/4 cup hot sauce

1/4 cup butter

1 dash garlic powder

1 dash ground black pepper

Directions:

1. Heat the oven to 350 degrees F.
2. Clean the chicken wings.
3. In a small bowl, combine the all-purpose flour, paprika, salt, and cayenne pepper or chili powder.
4. Place the chicken wings in a large glass bowl.
5. Coat the wings evenly with the flour mixture.
6. Cover the dish with plastic wrap, and keep it in the refrigerator.
7. Marinate for an hour or 90 minutes.
8. Spray a baking sheet with nonstick cooking spray (preferably Pam).
9. Place the marinated chicken wings on the sheet, and lightly spray the wings with cooking spray.
10. Bake for 45 minutes at 350 degrees F, then increase the oven temperature to 375 degrees F.

11. Take the wings out of the oven, and spray them with cooking spray.

12. Place the wings back in the oven, and bake them for another 10 minutes. This makes the wings crispy.

13. Make the sauce while the wings are baking. 14. Heat a saucepan over low heat.

15. Add the butter, hot sauce, ground pepper, and garlic powder, and stir them together.

16. Let the butter melt, and stir the mixture until it is well blended.

17. Remove the sauce from the heat, and pour it over the baked crispy chicken wings.

(Poem 3)

Balls Deep

Excuse me. Sweetheart, do you have a minute. I have something on my mind that I need to talk to you about. I'm not sure how this is going to make you feel, but I need to be 100 percent honest with you about a number of things that's been preoccupying my mind. There's a hidden message inside of what I'm about to say and I'm just going to maintain this secret between us until the day I physically leave this earth.

TRY not to focus on anything but us for the next few minutes. ALWAYS remember that nothing on this earth is more valuable than you. FLAIR your beautiful personality. FLAUNT the capacity of all you know. IMPROVISE the energy that would cause this perverse generation to recalibrate their values to manifest into a character that is honorable.

I have tried to describe you but because you are inexplicable, it seems I'm lost of what to say.
There are universal laws that are put in place
I have you in my heart
In this barometer, you will always be safe
We are part of each other
You are of a paramount importance
God's love is the most powerful element in practicing life in Christ
It cost me everything to operate in His love
This was my biggest sacrifice
But I know you're worth my time, my energy, and attention

I know I don't always say wise things and I'm open for corrections

Intensively, I meditate, thinking on multiple factors but sometimes I give up, asking myself, why does it even matter?

Meditation is something I do when thinking about you because I understand that there are realms of existence that have the ability to metamorphose reality

I wonder what it would be like to have you instantly appear here with me

Though you're not here yet, I'll see you soon enough

That's something I'm willing to bet but soon seems like forever

Soon is taking too long. I write about you in love letters, poems and songs to pass time until the day comes when we're finally in each other's presence and I hold you in-between my arms

Together, we are a storm

I'm like white fluffy clouds and you are the rain that
jumped on my back and rode me until I was dark
Heavy equipment in operation- we began to form sparks
Sparks that turn into more than just electric energies

The tempest of our whirlwind has somehow reformed
us
Transmuted from a storm to a hurricane called
Hennessy

We're storming and getting the world drunk from your
deep precious information. I'm going to interpret your
dark sayings and give them a revelation
Most people are not aware of the type of storm you are
You're not from this earth

The day you were born is when you descended from a stretch further than Mars. Your beauty has been wrapped around stars
I've always known you to be a great woman
Never ashamed for you to occupy an exclusive space
But in some ways, I'm still slightly afraid
I don't ever want to hurt you like I was hurt
That would be the craziest guilt
How could I ask for you to come closer without giving you permission to walk through the walls that I've built?
But emotionally, I want you to be in my life, in my world
My desires seem complicated - I've been through so many times of perils
Smiles are on my face in the day time but I'm dark and cold at night
I like it when it's dark
I can hide my pain better

I love when it's cold

I'll say things that probably shouldn't be told

A deep frost is on my bones but the thought of you has

been making me warm.

(Letter 3)

Don't Worry

Hey, my Love. I got something to put in your ear. There was this girl I met the other day. Her name is Hannah. She was telling me about some problems that she was having in her marriage. Her husband's name is Elkanah.

Ever since she was a child, she always wanted to have a family like everybody else. She got married and when her husband made love to her, they were excited because they were anticipating a child. Months passed and she was still the same size. She never got bigger. Her stomach remained the same and then she realized that no matter how hard they tried; she could not get pregnant. Her husband really wanted to have a child and when she saw his disappointment, she became extremely depressed.

Hannah was thinking of what she could do to make her husband happy again. She had a maid. Whatever she wanted, her maid took care of it. If she needed food, she would send her maid. If something needed to be cleaned in the house, her maid would take care of it. Swallowed up by depression, she suggested her husband have sex with her maid to have a baby. I know this sounds crazy but this is what really happened.

Then the maid became pregnant and gave birth. Hannah still wanted her husband to have more kids so she kept allowing the maid to have sex with her husband. She saw that the children were bringing him joy. However, her maid was provoking her - saying things to her that would make her feel even more depressed because she couldn't give her husband any children. The way she

was treating Hannah was not the character of a mother or friend. She became exceedingly sorrowful.
She didn't want to get rid of the girl who was bringing happiness to her husband. Seeing Hannah fade like the evening sun, Elkanah said, baby, why are you depressed? I love you more than 10 sons. Don't let this situation bring you down.

How that maid treated Hannah was disguised as a blessing because nobody knew that God was using this episode for His glory. Her maid was making Hannah so depressed and her soul vexed. Hannah was walking around, moving her mouth while no sound was coming out.

Day after day, she walked around with her head held down and while she was in depression and experiencing anxieties about her marriage, she depended on no one else but God.

Hannah wasn't convinced that her natural surroundings would get any better. She looked for a solution from natural resources within her household to bring joy to her husband to find that everyone in her house was experiencing happiness from her idea but apparently everything was turning against her. She wanted her husband back. How could something like this get this far out of control?

Hannah prayed saying, Lord, if you give me a child, I will give him back to you. How she felt has made God curious but what she said has caught His attention. Hannah, you are the first person in your generation to make this type of commitment. Then, a prophet named

Eli saw that she was moving her mouth but no words were coming out. He said woman, you are drunk. You need to stop all of that drinking. Hannah said, prophet, I wasn't drinking Bacardi. I'm not a child of Satan but I Am a servant of God and I'm just so depressed because I can't have any children. Eli prophesied to her saying that she would give birth to a son.

Baby, the reason why I'm writing you this letter is that I noticed that there are times I have things on my mind that bother you and you want to figure out what you can do to help. I just thought about their situation and wanted to tell you that everything is going to be alright between us.

From there, Hannah went home, took a shower, brushed her teeth, fixed her hair, and made herself smell good. She walked into her bedroom that night with a sexy lingerie Victorias Secret gown on and saw that her husband was laying across the bed, watching a movie, called American Gangster. She waited in the doorway until he looked up and noticed his wife was in a different mood. This was not the same woman he married. Something is very different about her. He didn't know exactly what it was but it's turning him on. He turned off the television, threw the remote across the room, and said, my love…I was thinking about you all day today. You're looking dangerously attractive right now. What's up? Hannah turned on some music by Barry White entitled Practice what you preach. Elkanah stood to his feet and said

So, what do you want to do?

I'm here, baby

I'm ready, baby

I'm waiting on you

Trust me, I am quietly waiting on you

In excitement, Hannah magically walked across the room. Elkanah also walked across and met her halfway to tell her

Sweetness

There's something going on with me.

Every time my mind thinks of you

I see your face in most of my dreams

Sweetness

You've done things that blew my mind.

Let's not do much talking baby

Let's not waste any time

I've had other lovers

They've said I was the best

And if you think I can't handle you

Just put me to the test

Girl you sneak

Dammm you a freak

In between the sheets

Telling me things

That you can do

Am I man enough to have time for you?

You said you have something you want to show me.

Here I Am sweetheart,

Practice what you preach.

Spice your lyfe

Spicy chicken wings recipe

These chicken wings are spicy and extremely tasty.

2 tablespoons parsley leaves, chopped small

Black pepper, to taste

1/2 teaspoon cayenne pepper

1/2 teaspoon onion powder

1/2 teaspoon garlic powder

1/2 teaspoon paprika

16 chicken wings

Butter spray

Directions:

Rinse the wings and pat dry with a small towel.

Turn on the broiler.

In a bowl, mix all the spices.

Spray the wings with butter spray on both sides.

Place the spices in a bag, and only add 3 or 4 wings at a time, depending on how big the bag is. Shake the bag with the wings in it to coat the wings.

Place the wings in a single layer on the broiler pan or a cookie sheet.

Cook for 2 minutes. Turn the wings over, and cook for another 2 minutes.

Do this 4 more times and then serve immediately. Once you serve it to your guest, read them this next letter, and get their response. Listen very closely to what they say and how they say it.

(Letter 4)

Brown Sugar

Sweetheart,

There are 7,655,957,369 people on earth.

3,730,000,000 of that population are women.

Solomon was the wisest man who ever lived. He had 700 wives and 300 concubines. His wives were daughters of kings. If a king wanted to start a war against Solomon, all he had to do was go to his wife, the king's daughter and say, baby, I need you to talk to your dad for me. Get him to calm down. He's acting like he's on his period, getting angry for no reason and it's not that serious. If it would've got really bad for any reason, what would the king do if he doesn't want any harm done to his daughter? It was forbidden for Solomon to marry outside of his nationality because these women would lead him astray from worshiping God to worship the gods that they worshipped. Over time, Solomon began worshipping Ashtoreth, who is said to be the queen of Heaven. The girls from Canaan worshiped this god, burning incense and making sacrifices to an idol that was said to represent the productive power of nature.

Solomon subsided from his place to worship Astarte / **Ashtoreth,** the goddess of the Sidonians. I believe she was referred to as the Queen of Heaven to whom the Canaanites poured libations. She was called a **goddess** of war and sexual love. If I was Solomon and I had to choose from over 3 billion women who I could marry and I only could pick 1,000 wives, I would definitely need you to be one of them. Then, if I had to get rid of 999 wives, you would have to be the one I keep because I believe that you carry a certain level of humility for us to learn from each other and grow together and become stronger. The purpose and reason I was born is more important to me than anything. Your humility has qualified you to be a woman that when God spoke and said "let there be light", anything He says proceeding that will fruitfully and productively come into existence and maintain the status of what He has spoken because the quality of your condition is good enough to sustain the Spoken Word of God. I said that to say, regardless of what I have ever done, you have to ask yourself what are my intentions?

I appreciate every female who looks at me as to be in a relationship or marriage because that means for them to see me in that capacity, they obviously value my characteristics and value me enough to want to invest their time in me.

Time is expensive, it is life. Once you give it, you don't get that time back but you can invest your time and get an experience that you can be glad to have for the rest of your life. We're investing our time into each other and I'm glad because the time I invest in you is nothing compared to what I'm getting in return. I appreciate you so much. I do the things I do because I enjoy the memories that we share together.

You were wise enough to identify my distinction and skills. Most women that I was caught up with wanted us to get married once we had sex because of how I was able to make them feel but they weren't able to identify what it was about me that was causing them to have the experience that they had. I am more than a moment of pleasure and good feelings. I'm a businessman, father,

Prophet, friend and I am a man. I'm confident in my distinction. My distinction is a weapon.

As crazy as it sounds, I've felt like I have been in relationships where I was compelled to compete with who I was with. The whole relationship seemed like a competition. I believe in compelling each other to move forward and go higher but only constructively. My destiny is different and I know that the woman who I choose to be in my life is going to have a tremendous effect on the motivation I need in fulfilling and maintaining the success of my purpose. I affect the world differently. There are 3 billion women on earth. I could give any one of them the opportunity to be with me but I only want you. I choose you.

Thoughts in Action

I imagine you on your front porch, enjoying dinner with Thunder, Rain, and your blanket. These are the names of people who have specific functionalities.

The front porch represents clearer skies and investments
It's a place of meditation for assessments
Thunder stimulates the emotions within yourself that when you speak,
you sound like the thunder of what you hear
The force of gravity and nature in itself is too much for one person to bear
So, you sit in that element and absorb the beauty that nature gives
You give rain to flowers that you come in contact with
Flowers reveal that you are beautiful
But they don't show you your true value

So, you wrap yourself in a blanket to allow your mind to go where your body can't

You close your eyes and feel the wind's voice, blowing through the blanket to get to your bones

Bones represent your soul

Your soul represents your life

Life represents our will

Our will represents our thoughts

Our thoughts represent where we are and who we want to be

I wanted to be under that blanket with you

I want to feel your energy

I'm closer to you than I think

But sometimes I don't think I can ever be close enough unless I become you and you become me

I keep seeing things

I saw something today

It's the same thing I saw about 6 years ago, and I've been praying the same thing, saying...God, please.

(Poem 4)

Fantasy Island

Baby, I want to hug you
It's one of the most powerful things I can do
I'm not perfect but my hugs are
I want to hold you in my arms and hold you passionately close
Generously giving myself to you-giving the most
I want to wrap you in my arms as if we were born as twins
For me to be separated from you is like one of the biggest sins
I want to love you so much that when I squeeze you,
and your breasts are pressed against my chest,
You will know the potential of our connection by understanding you are my best
You weren't my favorite until I hugged you

When we hugged and made that scintillating

Connection,

Something happened to me

When we hold each other's hands,

Our future is all I see

We are an icon

When we unite, we form a grip tighter than a python

I don't need to have sex with you in order to ejaculate

We can sit in front of a dancing ocean,

and burn for each other,

just because we are soul mates

I don't think like everybody

I'm different. I think for myself

I don't have to have sex with you to be intimate

but I have to be intimate to have sex with you

Giving me your body has to be something you're proud

to do

Your heart is connected to intimacy

Your heart isn't bulletproof,

So....you have to protect it...at all cost

In one split second, you can have your heartbroken

It may take years for it to recover

But I love you as if I was your father

I protect you as if I'm your big brother

Nobody is going to break your heart

Not even me

When I hold you, I'll hug you

When I hug you, I shield you. I enclose you

I block and protect anything from happening to you. I'm your protection. I'm your life insurance policy

I'm your lifeguard

I'll save you from drowning in deceit

I don't care if that means getting on my knees to serve you like the woman who cried at Jesus's feet

She washed the Messiahs feet with an expensive perfume
that cost what a person would have to work a whole
year to purchase
What she did is what I will do
You would never be worthless
You would never be wasted
You will never be rejected. You will never be accepted...
As some ordinary hoe.
You will never need to feel as if you're unnecessary
I know how real it is to struggle
But struggles crumble when we cuddle
...and I'm like an adult size muscular teddy bear
I'm soft enough to hold and strong enough to break
bones
I will fight for you if I have to.
If I have to physically fight in an all-out brawl,
Let me pave a path for you to escort you to the door. A
woman of your grade doesn't deserve to crawl

If I have to wake up at 3 am every morning and fight through my prayers,

I'm going to get you the victory just for the fact that I care

The danger is near? No problem

You don't have to worry

It's not your responsibility

I made sure I was prepared when I brought some utilities

I'm affectionate for the woman I love and you are the only one for me

(Letter 5)

The God System

Samuel was the king that God has appointed over Israel. Israel rejected Samuel because they wanted a king like the other nations. Little did they know they weren't rejecting Samuel. They were rejecting God.

They admired the structure of the systems of other countries that were delegated by their kings but as for Israel, the only system they had was God. The God system is far more advanced than human strategies but something in God's chosen people was causing them not to acknowledge what they had was far more superior than what they could get from another human being.

I'm mentioning this because sometimes, the distractions of our emotional surroundings direct us to other voices that don't lead us to what has been chosen by the voice of God. Ask yourself if you believe that it was God's plan and purpose for us to permanently grow together? If you believe this as I do, personally, I am sure that we should have more respect and honor for each other. Baby, I don't want to come home and look at you as if you're just somebody who lives with me. I don't want to look at you that way. I understand that most people would say that every relationship has problems, but what type of problems are we supposed to have? Are we supposed to cheat, curse, belittle, and fight each other? Are we supposed to sleep in different rooms away from each other at night? You may have done something that I didn't like. I'm sure you may not have been happy about some of the things that I've said and I'm not asking for a trophy, but we have to do an evaluation and work on ourselves.

I believe God sent us to each other. But how I treat you may determine if I can keep you. And that's not just enough because what we're intending to build requires us to be loyal. Furthermore, sometimes when you're raising your voice or complaining, I don't say nothing. I just stand there and stare, watching you talk. And before I respond to the energy you give me, I just go for a walk. Sometimes when I come back, you seem like you're still mad. I ask myself, am I really that bad?

In my conclusion, I peacefully say, if we should go our separate ways, and I decide to respect your wishes and leave, as a result of you rejecting me, make sure that you're not rejecting God. Make sure that you aren't releasing a permanent or temporary blessing that has been assigned to your life.

Before we met, you said that you deserved better, although many times, you've settled for less. If we want better, we got to do better. Which of my qualities do you find offensive? The value that you reject is the one you neglect. How could you expect to grow in honor and respect if you don't change certain ways that you have that result in the same effect?

Fight Night

Certified goon chicken wings recipe

Serves 12 (5 drumettes per serving)

Ingredients:

3 – 4 pounds chicken wings and drumettes, rinsed and patted dry

1/4 cup water

1 cup light soy sauce

Garlic powder (not garlic salt)

1-1/2 tablespoons fresh ground ginger or 1 tablespoon dried ginger

1-1/2 cups sugar or 3/4 cup sugar and 3/4 cup Splenda

Toasted sesame seeds

Heat your oven to 250 degrees F.

Cover a large baking sheet/pan, with heavy-duty aluminum foil.

Place the chicken the skin side, facing up across the baking sheet.

Sprinkle them with garlic powder, and set them aside.

In a medium-size bowl, combine the soy sauce, ginger, sugar, and water. Stir until the sugar begins to dissolve.

Pour the soy sauce mixture over the chicken, coating as much as possible.

Bake uncovered for 60 minutes, then turn the chicken over, and bake for another 30 – 45 minutes. Turn the chicken one more time. The teriyaki sauce will begin to thicken at this point. Continue baking and turning every 5 – 10 minutes until the sauce reaches a molasses-like consistency and is sticking nicely to the chicken. Total baking time should be approximately 2 – 3 hours.

The chicken can also be prepared in an electric frying pan or slow cooker, but the result is more caramelized and sticky-gooey when baked in a conventional oven. If you make them in a slow cooker, watch them closely so they don't overcook and fall apart.

Remove the chicken and sauce to a warmed serving plate. Garnish the wings with sesame seeds and then you and your boys start talking about girls of your past and what you liked and didn't like. Talk about who you would like to be with, who you want to smash and what y'all can do to step yo game up to become more confident to be with the one who you really want to be with.

(Poem)

Who am I?

When we met
I prophesied to you
Then you asked if we could be FRIENDS?
I said sure
A few days after, I had a vision that you had a MAN
I called you but didn't get through
Sent a message; asking if it was true?
You said yes
Then you started complaining to me how he treats you
Telling me that sometimes he treats you good…….
Other times, things go south and sometimes far west
He is unorganized in his plans and never does his best
He takes his frustrations out on you when a lot is on his chest

And worst of all

When you talk, he never listens

Growth and prosperity come from making the correct decisions

That's when you called me

We talked

I gave you advice

I let you vent and made you laugh

I encouraged and gave you information as a friend should do

You felt better after hearing my views

I told you to be patient

Ask him if he needs your assistance

You asked him

He said no

You felt the resistance

You called me back

Told me how he responded

Relax my friend

This doesn't mean you're in bondage

I said that to say

Sometimes

When brothers go through things

Things aren't always what it seems

Give him some time

It will get better and things will be fine

Little did I know

You were wishing to be mine

Concluding our call

In your head, you said, Wow;

I wish my man was just like you

I heard your thoughts but how I wanted to respond

wasn't the right thing to do

You called me the next day

Telling me what happened that night

You and your man got into the biggest of all fights
Y'all were supposedly making love
while kissing, eyes were closed
In your imagination, you saw my face and
Accidentally called him my name
He threw you on the floor and
Kicked you in your nose
You called the police and threw on some clothes
I never met this dude
But shortly after, I clearly understood he has a nasty attitude
You accidentally called him my name
I immediately understood why he would be mad
But he didn't have to hit & kick you as if you were a punching bag
He said it's my fault and says I was the one playing games
Don't do that bro. You don't want to feel this pain

I started to get upset

But I refused to step out of character

It's nothing for me to come scoop you like a spatula

I didn't want things to appear as if I was trying to get at this girl

I was only giving her the light of God's word and shining it in her world

I never intended for her to be enticed by my charming ways

God's love has put me in the 1st place of His stage

I know how and when to use my silver tongue

There has never been a time when I was scared to make these females run

I'm not saying that to catch interest or put on a show

But every time you hear my voice, your soul begins to glow

I try to hide as if I don't know

But I never left without adding color to your rainbow

Love comes to be tested and love comes with a sacrifice

Some say every woman has at least two men

I'm not about that life

I'm not going to lie

But in this situation, I refused to be the other guy

-Just a friend.

Tired of Thinking

You can NOT live without a brain

You can NOT live without a heart

You can NOT live without oxygen

but I """"CAN"""" live without you

I made it this far without you

I don't necessarily need you

I tried not to call yesterday to stay out of view

And not get in the way because I know you had

important things to do

but not talking to you for almost a whole day was not

easy

I love you so much and think about you all the time

I reserved a spot for you in my heart

Was that a mistake?

I literally don't know what's going on

I see things but I ignore

Some informational thoughts, I don't want to receive

What you tell me is the only thing I'm willing to believe

I love, want, desire and gotta have your black ass

I'm in need

My mind is programmed to eat from out of your hands

I fell to my knees

This mouth is open, ready for you to feed

Don't deprive me of your love or else I won't be able to breathe

When I expressed myself and told you I was starving

What does that mean?

It means I'm literally struggling for the light of your phone calls;

The oxygen of your presence;

The water of your voice;

The sound of your moans,

The taste of your skin

And the thoughts of us building something memorable

together...

But sometimes

Most times

And definitely a lot of times

I feel destitute

I'm jealous of prostitutes

They charge for their time

But mine is free and

I understand that you want to take it

But you can't

Because you're overwhelmingly busy

But I wait....

Patiently...

Quietly...

Hibernating in silence

And wait for these days

That we evacuate to tropical islands

To abandon the violence, pain, misery, and stress

Of not living my best

Because right now,

I can't say that I'm happy

living in a bubbled experience

Alone…

By myself without you.

(Letter)

Late in the night can be Late in Life

Good morning Queen. Thank you for your reply. I just called. I hope your morning is going well. It seems like my message rubbed you the wrong way. It feels like it did. When I say hygiene, I know you aren't walking around here stank. Lolz 🤣 🤣. I used the wrong word. I just woke up to use the bathroom and was about to go right back to sleep but when stuff isn't right, I worry a lot. Something told me to read my text before I sent it but I was like Nah...I'm going back to sleep.

I don't see you as a money-hungry hoe and neither do I see you as a dick hungry hoe. I'm not sure how you read my energy in my message but I was coming from a hopeless place of trying to hold on. I told you what I see you as. Sweetheart, I have explained that part to you more than once. ☹ You're right when you say that I'm not used to your pussy. Fucking is fucking but Sex and making love is more of a spiritual and mental experience than it is physical. I have been making love to you since the first day I met you. I was making love before our first kiss outside. Even, through our text messages, I was giving and giving and giving myself to you. I understand that love is giving. That's how I love. That's what I do. Do I want to have sex with you? Most definitely. I never want you to feel forced. Do I want to be with you and "build"? Duh...Of course, I want to build with you. Do I look at you as a sex toy and just wanna fuck? Most definitely NOT. I admit that I have been affected by the games of being played but I never got into a relationship and PLAYED, Cheated, or used females in a relationship as a rebound. My integrity and honesty are higher than that.

I was having casual sex with women since my first relationship - when I was 19. I was broken and then my last relationship, when I broke up with my ex in 2017, I declined every relationship and idea of marriage presented to me. I was so broken that I didn't want to live anymore. But if I just wanted sex from you, then my mindset wouldn't be like this, and I wouldn't feel the emotions I feel and I would never have given myself as I've done. It saddens/disappoints me that you said I wanted sex from the jump. When I read that part, I got STUCK and just put my phone down for about 20 or 30 seconds so I could regroup. I FAILED. When I'm in a relationship, I'm supposed to make my lady feel special. When I read your message saying I wanted to fuck when we first met, to me, it says Shawn, you don't make me feel special.

Do you remember that time when I asked you if I could be honest with you? You said yes. My exact words were

"I wanted to have sex with you when we first met but that's not my underlining driving force". I was overwhelmed and dazzled from all that I felt between us that I wanted to be CLOSER to you. Did you feel what I felt? I know you felt something. That energy means something. It's not just there to just be there. That energy is searching for two people who are willing to create a life together. Being closer to you is the ONLY reason why I wanted to take you on vacation and weekend getaways. I don't know the details of everything that happened to you before me but I've just been real and hope that we would eventually build something so good that's worth our time that outweighs all the bad that we've experienced from past connections.

I do feel great when I get my haircut - when I don't, I get very irritated. I don't think that you know what you mean to me and in your last message, it seems as if you took a huge step back, away from me. That shit is sad. I never wanted to use you or make you feel less or anything. And if I didn't care, I would still have been fucking other girls (if that was all that I was about). You are worth more than all that. You are more valuable. I'm not copying this of the Internet and sending it to you. I can't make this stuff up. It's all coming from a deep place in my heart. Seriously. I don't even know what to do now. To a certain degree, I can feel you and you don't have to say everything in order for me to catch on. I'm going to respect your space. I'm sorry for everything.

(Letter)

Sending you Flowers

When we were children, we always put everything in our mouth to understand what it is. When we look at something, listen to something, smell something or touch something, it is all activated by our sense of taste. When we taste, we know from within ourselves what the object is. Our parents would quickly remove stuff from our mouth because they don't want us to get sick, not realizing that the things they protect us from maybe the same moment they prevent us from learning. The truth is I may never know what a plastic cup tastes like, if I never drank water from a plastic cup; I may never know the difference between a plastic cup and a wooden toy with a plastic handle, if I never tasted it. Oh, taste and see!

A couple of decades later, I went back to the basic fundamentals to identify these objects

> Go to any Restaurant and ask five Guys. Baby, while I'm ingesting you and digesting your love for me, tears come to my eyes but I can't see them

but this time, they weren't made of plastic. They were made of multiple textures, juices, interior and exterior skin. Fornication has its own identity but nothing of this world can we name that taste better than sin. I'm ready to make my point. Shall I begin? Before I start, I just want you to know that this isn't about kids. Parental supervision is strictly advised. This is about how a grown man identifies and appreciates the quintessence of his woman.

In my conclusion, it is imperative that I politely give you this high priority message of letting you know that your pussy tastes better than the sunrise. I've opened my mouth and tasted the wind that blew down from sunny skies. Go to any Restaurant and ask five Guys. Baby, while I'm ingesting you and digesting your love for me, tears come to my eyes but I can't see them. Like Jay Z, I gotta let the song cry. My tongue activates every part of me. Suddenly, I reach forward, gently but firmly, squeezing your breasts and bringing my hands down to grip your cheeks. The activity of hearing the sound of you moaning my name isn't the same. Taste activated a sound-stimulating the desire and stirring the passion for me to often stick around to build a life with you. If we're in the kitchen or in my office, on top of the desk, there are things about you that make you taste the best. If we sat in the back center of a cinema and you grabbed my hand to put my fingers between your legs, putting my own fingers in my mouth, to tell me that this sweet juicy taste is called Yurina, should I believe it? We could be on a plane, in a dark park or at the zoo, i have plenty of things things to show you. There are plenty of things you would want me to do. These are a few reasons why I love being around you. You're the best girl in the whole world. The taste of you makes my toes curl. I even curl toes that I don't have. I'm not yet sure how to sum you up and what you do and how much you affect me in one word. It's the meticulous taste of your soul; the scintillating vibes exuberantly exhibited from your personality that liberates the lost forsaken passions of romance; the fire of your thoughts inspires a telekinetic moment of us to be in such a strong communication that causes us to wake up to each other's vibrations - Strong. Nothing or no one is comparable to you because you are the only you in the world and you are the only you who has ever existed and you are the only you that will ever be. And I'm not ashamed to say that I retrieved ALL of this information from the sweet delicious irresistible satisfaction of how good you taste.

(Poem)

My Love has No Expiration

When I was a little boy, I always felt this great energy

Never knowing exactly who or what it was called

But I kept breathing

I kept inhaling and exhaling

As a little boy on several paths

I was succeeding at some things

Other things I was failing

Today, I changed my perception about myself

I can't fail

I was learning

As I walked through the valley of the Shadow of life

I will fear no evil.

For thou art…

The gift of a woman I look to

Grant me the serenity to accept the things I can not change

Things were never destined to always REMAIN the same

But…

I keep breathing

I kept breathing until this energy was manifested from within me

As God brought Eve to Adam, I wondered if He brought you to me,

to see what I would call you

He breathed into me the breath of life. He gave me everything when He gave me his mind…

Then waited to see what I would call you

I called you on messenger but you didn't pick up

I didn't call your cell and I won't ask for your number

If that's something I deserve, suggest it to me

And depending on how you say it

I may portray it as a sign that the doors are open for you to be mine

And to begin building this LEGACY

IF YOU WERE MINE,

I WOULD practice on you,…….

Like a Guinea pig,…….

And cut you open,…….

To pull out all possibilities of fears, insecurities and any form of worry

I want to operate on you with your full permission that this love will give you the hope to see…….

Your son

Baby my love has no expiration.

Prophet Passion can tell you exactly where he is

What he's doing at this second

And create a way for you to see your kid

I don't think it is a coincidence that this thought came to mind

I believe the the answer is here

And not only is God making a way for you to see your son

Be with your son and have your son

But I see some things happening for you

That will lead you into having full custody

One of the reasons my heart goes out to you is because it seems that your son is me

I went through a similar thing

Because I was literally adopted at the age of 3 and I don't know my biological mom or dad

I'm not really aware of the whole situation

Perhaps there could have been a De-escalation
I believe being a foster child was a better decision for my incarnation
And God had a perfect plan of a Crisis intervention to bring a miraculous life changing transformation

I'm not telling you that you might see him or it's a possibility
I'm prophesying to you again for the second time to let you know that God made a way for your son to be in your life again
I prophesy it; I decree it and speak it right now, in Jesus name. Amen.

Appointed for Sweetness

Prophets are the voice of God
We are known to be a special part of the body of Christ
But around those who think they know us, sometimes
we are the least esteemed
A prophet is not without honor except by his relatives
and in his own country
We play interesting roles in the scene
But many prophets misuse and abuse their gift
Some lie and others move swift
We can prophesy in an instance, on the drop of a dime
Some of us are used in healing
We can recover the sight of the blind
Some of us can dance
Some of us are in clubs
Watching girls twerk
Some of us are in the marketplace

Inspiring those at work
A few of us are on the streets, chilling in the hood
We bring comfort and watch people grow
From low income neighborhoods to Hollywood
Some of us are in churches and some of us are attorneys
Some of us move quickly and will walk you through your journey
Every Prophet is not the same
We all don't operate from the same gift
When we look weak
Jesus Christ is our strength
There's nothing in this world we can't lift
We don't always operate the same
But our gift comes from the same Spirit
He elevates us above pain
Some of us are comical and others sarcastic
At times, we're under so much pressure
And other days, feeling fantastic

We don't all have the same personality
We're not all of the same nationality
We come from different backgrounds and different ethnicities
But we wrestle against spiritual darkness in high places
We dethrone principalities
Some of us deal with romance, sex, marriage, love and families
Some are a part of the educational system
We see those in need and show His true charity
Apostles are represented as lions but Prophets are eagles
We're prophetic birds
Some of us are poets
We specialize in spoken words
There are over 60 different types of eagles;
Pygmy eagle
Southern banded snake eagle
Pallas's fish eagle

Sandford's sea eagle

Crested hawk eagle

Crested serpent eagle

Martial eagle

Stellers Sea Eagle

Baldheaded eagle

Golden eagle

There are so many different types of eagles

We can never be put into a box

We are not designed to mimic other species

We'll grow out of a cage and bust lucks open

Every one of us is different and not always designed to

fit in

We're designed to please God

We came on earth to win

Made to fly

That's why we fly high

That's why we refuse to give up

That's why we refuse to die

Jesus is the reason we spend so much time in the sky

No matter how hard the confrontation, we're designed

to rise

Our needs are always supplied

From God's Grace, we can't hide

It's Him who appoints

It's Him who qualifies

It is Him that justifies

When we meet people who needs God's love,

All we do is apply

In God, we trust

In God, we confide

We live in the secret place of the most high

Under His shadow is where we Abide.

My mind is soaked

Hey my sweet lady. I want to take our relationship to a higher level. For years, I remembered this scripture but never really understood what it meant.

Deep calls unto deep, at the noise of thy waterspouts. All I knew was deep calls unto deep, until I recently got a revelation. If I'm deep and I say something deep, only deep thinkers will be able to understand what I've said.

A man's mind is as deep waters but only a man of understanding can draw it out. So, your mind is deep but if you don't have the understanding of how to get that information out of your mind, into reality, you're like a huge powerful train that should've moved, could've moved, would've moved but never moved. Movement is an indication of life and revelation gives you the ability to move.

If two people are racing, both of them are obviously alive and neither of them are more alive than the other but one person has a revelation which permits him to possess the skill that will cause him to be able to run faster than the other. That skill comes from information. Information will reveal what you need to do in order to move. As you apply the understanding, you become better at that movement and you will be able to perform that movement faster. The information will assist you in creating a program for effective training. It may consist of stretching, restrictions of foods you eat, how many times you eat, what time of the day you eat and how much sleep you get. Both runners are running but both are experiencing different results.

Two people can work for the same corporation, have the same title and work in the same office but get results which in the process of time reveals that one person has a more astute understanding of how to transpose his ideas into a lifestyle.

A man's mind is as deep waters...but a man of understanding knows how to take the information of that water to implement it from a thought, to an idea and to reality.

Deep calls unto deep at the noise of thy waterspouts. What is a spout? A spout is a tube or lip projecting from a container, through which liquid can be poured. So, when I think of a spout, I think of a faucet. When you turn on your kitchen sink, water comes out. If you turn the water up high, you will hear the sound of the water falling to the bottom of the sink and you can also hear the sound of it coming out of the spout/faucet. So, this tells us that the waterspout of a

> The word of God says that a man's mind is as deep waters but a man of understanding knows how to turn on the faucet so that the water can come out

kitchen sink has a sound. If you turn the sink very low until only a drop of water falls from the faucet once every few seconds, you may not be able to hear it in the faucet. You will be able to hear the sound of that drop of water fall into the sink and that will be all. But when you turn the sink on high for the water to come out at full speed, the water receives a revelation, which enables it to move a lot faster than it did before and the sound of the water released from the waterspout is an indication that the water is coming from a deep place. It's coming from a place of deep waters. The word of God says that a man's mind is as deep waters but a man of understanding knows how to turn on the faucet so that the water can come out.

So baby, what I'm saying is this; that waterspout is us. Jesus said that from the abundance of the heart, the mouth speaks. The abundance of the heart is the mind and the mind is the abundance of deep waters and we speak but we haven't always spoken from the deep things of the spirit. From our belly will flow rivers of living waters. Without a doubt, we are more spiritual than natural but we have been living in the natural realm for so long that we have become blind and desensitized to things of the spirit.

When the word of God said that when Jesus spoke, his voice was as many waters, it means that he spoke from a revelatory deep place of knowledge, wisdom and understanding.

Jesus walked on water and when the storm came, he rebuked the wind because water represents revelation. If you have revelation, you have wisdom. When you have wisdom, you have an understanding of how to use the information of knowledge you know. As a waterspout, you have been enabled to speak the words of life from a deep place of refuge, abundance and every resource at the disposal of the Kingdom of God.

We are like a tree planted by the rivers of living water. Why does the word of God refer to us as a tree planted by "living" water? It's because God has made us to absorb that water (information/revelation). We absorb the revelation and when we open our mouth to speak, we release a deep sound that only those who are spiritually mature may be able to understand.

1 John 5:8 -11 says that there are three that bear witness in earth, the Spirit, and the water, and the blood: and these three agree in one. And this is the record, that God hath given to us eternal life, and this life is in his Son. This clearly shows you how important this water is. Out of all of the things in this world, water is one of the most powerful things that we can possess. Water is knowledge and revelation. It is a unique powerful substance. It is something that can be used by us to take our relationship to an entirely higher and deeper level in God, and I'm thirsty for this living water so that we can go higher and deeper in His Spirit.

Freak Fest

Serves 6 (4 – 5 drumettes for each person)

3 pounds chicken wing drumettes

2 teaspoons salt

1/4 cup olive oil

1/4 cup tequila

1/2 teaspoon freshly ground black pepper

1/4 teaspoon paprika

2 garlic cloves, minced

1/4 cup onion, finely diced

3/4 teaspoon ground cumin

1/4 teaspoon dried thyme leaves

1 tablespoon fresh cilantro or parsley, chopped fine

4 limes

Wash and pat dry the chicken wing drumettes. Place the drumettes in a glass or plastic container, arranging them in a single layer.

Combine the tequila, olive oil, salt, black pepper, garlic, onion, thyme, cumin, paprika, and cilantro. Stir well, and drizzle the resulting marinade over the chicken drumettes.

Roll the limes on a hard surface. Cut them in half, and squeeze the juice directly onto the drumettes. Cover, and marinate them in the refrigerator for 2 hours. Turn the drumettes, and marinate them for 2 more hours or overnight.

Approximately 1 hour before serving time, heat your oven to 400 degrees F. Roast the drumettes uncovered for 50 minutes, basting every 10 – 15 minutes.

For extra-crispy drumettes, place them under the broiler until they reach the desired crispiness.

Once they are crispy enough to your satisfaction, let them freaks know what time it is.

(Poem)

I Need You

I'm going to try to be straight forward regarding what I think and how I feel

I don't want to ever imagine myself as fake

I'm empowered when I'm real

You are special and you know that you are

That's a great accomplishment that brought you far

You know that you're special but are you special to me?

The answer …….

Yes, you are

But thoughts replayed in my mind regarding a recent message you sent

You plainly said you don't need nobody…

To basically say, you would appreciate anything that I may do for you

But you don't need me

That was the message I got and maybe I read wrong-

between the lines

Maybe I misunderstood when you told me to stop

telling you that you look fine

I see things through my eyes.

I speak from my heart

I interpret things from my mind.

I'm far from blind.

I knew what I was doing

I want to be needed

If I feel like you don't need me

I'll feel like you don't want me

You were my priority

And in the midst of your busyness

I was patient

Patiently waiting

But anxious for my queen to grace me with her presence

As I fall to my knees...

To honor you, love you and need you

As if my life depended on it

Making you the most special woman in my world

Is equivalent to making you my woman-my girl

Because

When I'm in a relationship

I put My Queen on a pedestal, always

But as I explained the other day

When I'm hurt

I feel dumb and so stupid…

Abandoned and left alone

I feel like a fool

Because there have been times I've said

If the light is not green and the flags red

I wont love and trust again because that would create no end of a war in my head

Beauty is in the eye of the beholder

I beheld you

My love is as sincere as a child's

Now I'm older

Would you believe me if I tattooed your name on both shoulders?

I "NEEDED" you and I told you this

More than once

I expressed that when I said

Part of me has fallen in love

Maybe you didn't feel it that way

Maybe you didn't know how to believe it could be that way

But my hopes were that things would eventually lead to us growing that way

I was hungry for you to be a part of my Change

Love gives

So, the most valuable thing in my possession I could release to you was myself

I gave that and everyday

I was psychologically giving you more and more of me

My hormones never once got in the way

It's all inclusive

Breathing is a part of me; it empowers my hormones

Eating is a part of me; it affects my emotions, sexuality and self esteem

These are essential desires

But also needs

It doesn't get in the way

But would it be hard to understand?

That my body parts, desires, mental and spiritual aspects

Are all a part of who I Am?

It was apart of what I was offering

This is more than just feelings

This is my life

My life has been given to you, so it was yours

But you gave it back, and it became ours

The time and interest I give you

Are the flowers I give

These flowers, I gave you every day

Even now, after feeling rejected

In someways, the pain of it makes me feel less than disrespected

But how can I be happy if I'm not accepted by the one I love?

If she has not assured me that my heart is protected

I want you

I still do but what can I do with you?

All I wanted was to be connected

But maybe that was more than what I should have expected

I'm a horny, loving, fun, outgoing, romantic, soft, kind hearted, passionate freak

A king that wants to show you how much you mean to him

I want to give you a peak

Of real love that will put you to sleep

Wake you up by sweeping you off your feet

To let you know that this is not a dream

Not just for now but for eternity

I'm always this sweet

I'm always nice

I'm always romantic and full of surprises

Would you take me every time I give myself to you?

I have a lot of love...a lot

But if I wake it up

Who's going to be responsible to entertain these characteristics?

When it's awake

It takes a long time to put this blazing fire to rest

If you're not ready for this love

You'd have to plan it
This love will make you feel like you're out of this planet
If you reject it by not accepting it
The blazing flame minimizes down to a flame
Then down to a spark
Then silently it sits in the corner of my heart
And tells me
Don't wake me up for a woman who's going to fold
I'm the type of fire that wants to love out of control
I want to burn everything across my path - everything in sight
Next time, please be sure to find the queen
Who is greedily and anxiously ready to receive all of Mr. Right.

Round 3

Knock out Buffalo chicken wings recipe

3 pounds chicken tenderloins or wings, skinned

1/2 cup Frank's RedHot Buffalo Wings Sauce

1/2 cup Frank's RedHot Original

In a big pot, boil the chicken for 15 minutes.

Don't let the chicken fall off the bone.

Remove the wings from the water.

Wait for them to cool until they're easy to manage.

Carefully pull the skin from off each piece.

Use a baking dish to mix the two sauces, add the chicken, and stir it evenly.

Cover the wings, and bake for 30 minutes at 350 degrees F.

Remove the cover and stir it.

Bake for an additional 10 minutes while it's still uncovered. Set your timer and go look into the eyes of your divine feminine and tell her how important she is to you. When the timer goes off,

put the wings on a plate with some ranch dressing or blue cheese dressing on the side with some celery sticks and a cold picture of Kool-aid with pineapple chunks on ice.

(Letter)

Prioritize

Baby, I want to prioritize you.

Earlier, I was thinking about you. I was thinking about me and I was thinking about us. I was thinking about what type of chemical reaction we make when we're together. I was wondering what people see, different from what we feel. Do they see what we feel? I'm not sure if I want to manifest what they feel or see because as we know, there are men who want you and there are women who want me and a lot of women wanted to be in the position that you're in because I have learned to treat a lady really well. I appreciate you. I know women were made to be man's help but there's a difference between you helping me and you doing something while I sit back and watch. I barely can allow you do anything for me because it just feels weird. I'm not used to having women do stuff for me. I've had some hard times in my life where I struggled to barely survive, while there were women who wanted to basically take care of me. That would be like Heaven for a lot of men because they are tired but despite the tiredness, some of us still won't take this route because we're built to last. We're born soldiers. We can be very clean as well as dress to impress and even smell nice but we're never scared of getting our hands dirty. I will crawl through the mud on my face, if necessary. I'm not bragging. We all have gifts and can always tell other people how to solve their problems but we often don't know how to free ourselves. By the grace of God, I don't have that problem. I know how to work and I also know how to wine and dine. I know what to

> I know how to work and I also know how to wine and dine. I know what to do to make sure you're fine

do to make sure you're fine. Once, you were in line, waiting until it was your turn. The first thing I said made your heart burn. That's how you knew I was the one for you. Because not every man can put a smile on your face. Neither can every man be stern and put you in your place when you get besides yourself or get out of hand. And not every guy knows how to be your man and your friend. So, what is it that you like about me, besides my wide shoulders, strong chest, abs and biceps? I know you love my sense of humor. I make you laugh all of the time. I know how to hold conversations while giving feedback. There are times when i let you vent but you are my help. You help me in ways that I need most and the only thing I require is the same thing you've been doing since the first day I looked into your beautiful brown eyes.

Just keep smiling and being an optimistic person.

(Poem)

White lies & white lives

Imagine if our ancestors went to Europe
Hurled thousands of innocent white people
Kidnapped them
Put them on a boat
And took them to a country that we stole - America.

Imagine if we put them on a farm
To plant tobacco and harvest our crops
Waited days before we fed them and watched them starve

Imagine if we made them go outside to drink from dirty sinks
That has a sign, saying "whites only"
Telling them, your name is Kunta Kenta

Not Tobe

Imagine if they built Wall Street and their blood was washed down those streets
Imagine if we raped their wives in front of their children and husbands
And the slave owners were called niggers

Imagine if Donald Trump was the only white president that America ever had
Imagine if black people were really bad
Imagine if everything they've done to us
We did to them

Imagine if we demoralized their men

Imagine if all of the white racist people were in the middle of interstates, highways and on each corner
screaming
White lives matter

It ain't over till the fat lady sings
But She's in the drive through of KFC
Getting fatter
While angrily ordering a meal from a 16-year-old, black employee

Imagine if we invented the Willie Lynch system and devised an idea to turn white people against themselves
To cause white women to not respect white men
Because he could never be a...black man
And he doesn't have the necessary equipment of what it takes.......to be black

He can't endure the sun

He doesn't have the muscle

He doesn't have the voice

He doesn't have the brain

He doesn't have the charisma to make his woman go insane

He doesn't know what it's like to really love a queen so he plots on the murder of Dr. King...

And the reason """"Y"""""

He doesn't like Malcolm X

Is because he's so focused on ZZZ or the KKK

Black people don't have a history of murdering whites

Regardless of what they may say

But today, white people have a history of murdering black people

In our society, we're still racially profiled
When all we've ever asked for is a system that's equal
But the oppressing racist cracker has always been afraid
of Kings and Queens
To get into office and to make decisions about
education, health care and the implementation
of welfare
They have been traumatized by their own nightmares

And after whipping us, burning down our houses and
churches, spraying us with fire hoses, gunning us down
and having their knees in our neck
They got the nerve to tell us to peacefully protest

Some of them went on social media and told me that I'm
a man of God
And if I'm like Jesus, I should learn how to forgive and
forget

They want us to wear the shoes that they despise to
walk in
BUT STILL OPPRESS.

They're not the ones who are worried about their kids
Coming home from a party
Being pulled over by law enforcement
And it turns to police brutality
In fact,

The police is not riding up and down their streets
Stopping them
Frisking them
Asking for their ID

Imagine if the shoe was on the other foot
And they went through everything that we went
through historically

And robbed them of their culture
Changed their language
Changed their names
Humiliated them in front of their families
Never allowed them to rewrite our bible
And we remained
The black King James!!

What would life be like in America??
But you know what?
If black people were in power
We wouldn't do that to white people
Because it's not apart of us to be that evil

The same way they genetically modified foods made in the lab
Is the same way they genetically modified and imputed sin into our brothers and sisters

To circulate evil among ourselves into our communities
And being vulnerable to their tactics
We did what we were told
In order to survive

None of this should be a surprise
To be a white racist is to tell white lies
Where your heart is puffed up
And so full of pride

Imagine, if their history was compromised
And their forefathers were hand-carved
Made into ornaments
And hung from Christmas trees
Surrounded by lights for the whole world to see

Imagine if Breonna Taylor was Britney Spears
And

George Floyd was George Washington or Elvis Presley
And the police had his knee on their neck for eight
minutes and 46 seconds.
Imagine that!

Three, Two, One

Sweetheart, if I was with you right now, I would either cook for you or take you out for dinner tonight. I would then run your bath water and help you get in while playing soft sensual music. As you soak in this bubble bath prepared by the choicest, I would place a gentle kiss on the side of your head. Then, I would unleash another weapon in my arsenal - exclusive, deep tantalizing poetry. As my mouth utters each word in great affection, my hand will wash you with a customized sponge marinated in exotic fruits and soaked in a peach fragrant body wash.

Omg... baby. I want you so bad right now! I'm outside of the hospital in Alexandria, Virginia. waiting for a patient but I really want to make love to every drop of you very slowly. After your bath, I will dry you off with a luxurious 100% Cotton towel with small linen ruffles around the edges that are barely felt and seen. We both will realize that I have committed to be the man that travels to the other side of the country to carry you in my arms and exit you from the bathroom, through the dining room, across the hallway and finally to the bed...as I reach into the draw of my nightstand and pull out a $259 8oz bottle of oil which possesses an acquired scent. I apply it to your feet, ankles, legs, thighs, pelvis, hips, stomach, breasts, arms, shoulders and neck. Then I'll flip you over, starting from the top of your neck and working my way down towards your waist and massaging the dimples on your soft, delicious ass, diving in, (tongue first), I begin to kiss and lick the inside of your thighs and tasting the juices of everything that God has rained inside of you... I'll tease you but when I slowly start giving you this hard, thick,

> I begin to kiss and lick the inside of your thighs and tasting the juices of everything that God has rained inside of you

irresistible D, I'm going to connect with you in a way that no one has ever had the understanding of how and I am going to give it to you so good that when I pull out, it will still feel as if I'm in every part of your body..... You will feel like you're living outside of yourself, watching me as your Yoni feeds me the sweet cum that I will swallow with unspeakable joy.

Baby I wish I was there to be sipping from you as if you were a hot cup of Hibiscus tea.

Sixty Six Angels

I don't want an ordinary relationship

If I'm going to have something, it should be something that I enjoy

> I'm about to flow in the spirit by singing a worship song. I'm going to manifest a spark and fan it with my worship

It should fit my personality and God's will. It should be a replica of what's lovely in the spirit realm. It should be a tangible explosion of what we would want to experience on a regular basis. It should be something that we shouldn't have to compromise our values for. I got an idea. Let's worship with the angels. Lock the windows. Shut the doors and let the game begin. I'll be the one to initiate this experience since it's my idea and I'm the one who appears to be so eager to acquire this. Watch me as I give God the fruit of my lips. Wait for 66 seconds before you open your mouth or do anything. I'm about to flow in the spirit by singing a worship song. I'm going to manifest a spark and fan it with my worship. As I do, 66 seconds later, I want you to join in and sing. While you join in, I'm going to shift and start praying - EXALTING THE NAME OF THE LORD.

After 77 seconds, you keep singing, sing and invite the angels in. Omg baby, when you invite the angels in, I'm going to recite scriptures, rebuking the enemy - cutting off any influence of interference that he may have, disallowing him to distract us from creating an atmosphere for God to live in. Just keep singing- worshipping God. I'm shifting from rebuking the Satan and his cohorts to now reciting scriptures to reverence God. The angels are worshiping with you baby. They are dancing with you and waving with you, floating around with you and bowing down with you. We have a ministry of angels and all we're doing is inviting them to participate in our worship, as we change our atmosphere around us into the atmosphere from within us.

Now

When I talk, please don't say a word until I'm finished

But when it's your turn to talk, speak up

There are things in your mind that I need to know

I Am one of the elites

I'm Highly intelligent

Extremely confident

Eminently successful

I represent about 76% of all senior executives

Naturally, I Am a leader

I willingly embrace various levels of responsibility

And although I possess quintessential strengths, I Am humble and easy to work with

I am expected to preside in the bedroom

And in a business setting, I can easily dominate your conference room

I'll fill every square inch of its space with

utter certitude and power

I'm a genuine leader who you could envision by your side

Leading you into a safe place that's sweet, not sour

Don't wake up in a nose-to-nose argument with me

Don't let that mistake happen as a result of you being invariably irate and emotional

It won't end pretty for you

You will regret the outcome

If you can see into the future

You would avoid those unpleasant encounters

I Am a great person to have on your team because I am your commander

I Am Your visionary

Your strategist and executor

I Am tougher than red meat

Your secrets and life are safe with me

They won't be leaked

Don't misunderstand the consistency of my personality

for anything that is inappropriate;

My confidence isn't arrogance

My toughness isn't belligerence

Though my competitiveness can be interpreted as a fight

to the death

Working with me is easy

I'm dominant, confident and love to take charge

I Am aggressive and competitive

I Am incredibly task focused

I Am bold and innovative

I Am persistent and steadfast

Knowing exactly how to engage with me

Will determine if you have what it takes to last.

Access

Adam knew his wife. One of the greatest things about sex is the connection because information comes from the connection, which causes you to know something that you didn't know before. Adam knew his wife. That means, He received information from her. He had access to her experience. He had access to her atmosphere. He had access to her environment. He had access to her soul. He had access to the way she thinks, what she thinks, what she feels, how she feels it, the decisions she makes and when those decisions are made.

As men, most of us don't understand how much further we could go by having access to a woman. Simply looking at a woman is a distraction because all we see is what our eyes can see but rarely do we view her, according to the eye of the mind, or as we may call it, the eye of our understanding.

> But my problem has always been that I fall in love fast

So, when I say that I want to taste you or if I'm making gestures that I want to be deep inside of you, it's really as Adam knew his wife. I want to know you too! Baby, I want to know you like no one has ever known you.

It's a good thing to be in love but I've fell in love with the wrong women. That was always my biggest problem. Are you a part of the problem or a part of the solution? I confess that I have given love where it's not valued or appreciated and some may say that I didn't love them more but I had a better way of showing it. Well, if it's in our heart but we don't show it, is it still love? Maybe we can keep that love to protect ourselves but that method of protection may be the physiological error that keeps us bound to repetitive cycles, over and over again. We'll attract different people with different birthdays and different ethnicities and different backgrounds and different occupations and get the same results every single time. This could be a result of having sex with the wrong person because every time you have sex with someone, you're learning something. You're downloading information and softwares and viruses that can cause you to shut down in the middle of all of the work you've uploaded but none of it will be saved, everything will be deleted. Your world has crashed and the little bit of virtue you had is now depleted because of a connection you should have never made. Every man is not designed to know you. It's not meant for you to exchange sexual information with someone who has a nice smile or good personality. Adam exchanged information with Eve. He knew her. She knew him and I want to know you in the deepest passionate way possible. I want to use my tongue to write heavenly languages All Across the walls of your vagina. "MENE MENE TEKEL UPHARSIN"

I am counting the days of your misery

And bringing it to an end.

Every perpetrator and fraud that has lied to you have been weighed but does not measure up to what they promised.

They have been divided against themselves and finally, you have been given to me.

So, let's start this off right between us. We're both grown and what we do in our private time is absolutely nobody else's business but ours and the only thing I want is to know you inside and out. I want your full permission, cooperation and access to know you as I give you full and complete access to me and what I have to offer.

A King's Love

Is it possible to be in love with two women at one time?

Every man has two men inside his mind

A King and a fool

My king was in love with Lisa

But my fool was in love with Bri

My charming, seductive ways

Has picked two girls that were ready to play

We were in the club

But only two came into VIP

Lisa was dancing as Bri would sing

Everybody else left to go home

It was just us three

I sat in the chair

Watching the way she moves, I felt fire in my chest

But in my peripheral view, I was looking through foggy smoke and saw Bri's silhouette

That girl assumed the position to give me a slow neck

My fool was falling in love

The king was not blind.

Two women getting the best of my world at the same time

Pouring my money into each slot machine

I hit the jackpot from behind

This was for nobody else

It was only mine

A man's dream come true

We slept in my bed, King size

I did some king-sized things

One sat on my lap and the other sat on a place where I couldn't see

I stayed beneath her until she heard me saying "I can't breathe"

Afterwards, Lisa was on my left

Bri was on my right

Lisa was wet and loose

Bri was tight and right

They never worried about me slipping

They were on each end; giving me the best rides

We were closed in an open relationship of wet water slides

Bri's my accountant

She's good with numbers and sings like a god

Lisa is good with networking

Her net worth is displayed in marketing

We did everything together

Went to church

Went to clubs

We went shopping together and if I spent too much money on Bri

Lisa said don't worry boo, I can take care of me

We had an understanding

We were becoming ONE family

Sometimes I didn't have enough money for their spree

No man can serve two masters

He would love one and hate the other

Lisa is chocolate

Bri is vanilla

We were between the same sheets and under the same covers

They were like sisters who took care of each other

Calling me Poppi Daddie. Sometimes Mister

I'm never cheap with them

I never cheat on them

They are all I need and I mean, my girls are the greatest team

Her Stage name is Lisa but everybody calls her Bri

I'm just a king and there's a fool in me...

Ready to fall in love!

Easy for life

It's a good thing when a woman has a man who is

willing to help her

That's why I'm here

You struggle to balance everything

And still, try to remain pretty

Many women have said

If a man won't accept me for the way I Am

He can just go find another girl

With this type of mindset, how do you expect to impact

his world?

Is that an excuse to settle for where you are?

And as soon as he comes across your path

He turns right back around

When you call him

His phone makes a different sound

If he's like me, he will save your number

When you call, his phone says "RUN"!

That's what you're saved under

Is he trying to avoid you?

Why do married men go to strip clubs?

Why do some men cheat on their wives?

Why cheat on the one you love?

This happens all the time

Men, we love being entertained

Enjoying ideas that stimulate our brain

After work, we'll let time fly away with friends

Just to drink and smoke from the beginning of the day to the end

What do we want?

We want sex. We need it

We want to feel important. We need it

Our bodies are designed for this but

Most of us have no idea, how challenging it is...

To be a woman

There are standards that we've set for you
It may be high but if you try, these standards can be
lived up to
Being a woman is a lot of work
More than most men may ever realize
And then if she's a single parent, having a child alone is a
job that's full time.

War in a Bottle

Let's take a moment to put everything aside
So, I can look into your deep mysteries - eyes right now,
To tell you
That you are special to me

I published a book of love letters, poetry, inspirational quotes, and chicken wing recipes.

Could you ignore me if all I bring is peace and hope?
You won't be able to keep my name out of your mouth.
I'm deep in your throat?

My occupation - research analysis.
I went from the end to the beginning
Like revelation to Genesis
I work full time in horticulture

investing in dreams that you won't resist

This is a part of my career

When you met me, I had power

I am a commander of atmospheres

May you ever be intoxicated with my love

I am your lover

Spread your legs for me

I will blow on your garden

That the delicious scent of what you reserved for me may spread abroad

The mist of it all comes from your radical thoughts

I will go into you and taste your choice foods

Once, I was a child, I told my Father,

When I walk up to her, with my shiny shoes and navy blue suit,

My mouth will be saturated with clusters of her fruit

I will put my hand by the entrance of her door

The movement of my fingers will make her want me
more
I'll give her 12 roses, directly handed in her chest
Let her smell the fragrances
There are different stages
Inside of her, I'm in different places
God was the first person to plant a garden
Relax as I display my floral designs
I believe that you would like this surprise

My education, conservation, and psychotherapy
contribute to your deep sleep
Flowers are born to express emotions that you have
never felt
But will do almost anything to keep
I know how to express myself through flowers, without
saying a word

Some flowers will always attract specific birds

My flowers attract you

As soon as you walk in

You'll enjoy the view

The door is decorated with the **Lily of the Valley**

Nothing about this moment will turn into a tragedy

Lilies are the world's second most expensive, uniquely shaped, white color flower

As my love, there are some things I may require

Commonly, Lilies grow in the mountainous areas

You'll be stunned by its beauty

The price tag is delirious!

Let's go a little further

Things just got serious

The Kadupul flower is probably the most expensive flower in India but it is only able to survive the night

Internationally, it is known for its calming sensations
from its fragrance insight
Worldwide, It is known for its amazing qualities
Inhale the aroma of my presence
Let's create new policies
If you really want my presence to fill your room
I'll grab you a bottle of Epi-phyl-lum Hook-eri perfume
There is nothing good in this world that I wouldn't bring
to you
I'll bring treasures at your feet
I'll bring you Roses, Shen-zhen Nong-ke Orchid
Not just once but I'll repeat
Saf-fron cro-cus and the Gold of Kin-a-balu Orchid
Bright lights fill our room. Ideas has been exported.
My Hyd-ran-gea comes in mainly white blooms
But I'll give you pink, light purple, violet and blue
I'll give you the Li-si-an-thus blooms
With me, you'll have options

And travel with me to warm regions like Mexico, southern united states, northern South America and the Caribbean

Let me overlay your body with the striking colors of large, oval petals and make you moan this weekend

When I surround you with the colors of white, purple, lavender, blue and violet

Get your passport and be ready to select your pilot

We can travel to the city of romance

Experience café culture

I'll hand feed you rich chocolate and the finest of wines

Introducing exciting sight-seeing adventures above and below the skies

As we feel images of the iconic Eiffel Tower lit up at night

We'll experience the best luxury amenities

With a full staff including a chef, butler and two nannies

A beachfront villa in Jamaica

You'll meet Mr. Kulan

He is my private wellness and mindfulness trainer

For me to make you happy is a no brainer

I'm ready baby

Are you?

Made in the USA
Columbia, SC
10 April 2025